Step-by-step
Découpage

Step-by-step
Découpage

Letty Oates

CAXTON EDITIONS

This Edition Published 2000 by
Caxton Editions an Imprint of
The Caxton Publishing Group

Copyright © 1995 Regency House Publishing Limited

ISBN 1 84067 1181

Printed in Hong Kong.

Contents

Introduction

Découpage is the craft of decorating objects with paper cut-outs and varnishing them until the effect is of hand painted images beneath a heavy lacquered surface.

Découpage as a pastime is quite inexpensive. Cut-out images and motifs can be taken from magazines, books, cards and gift wrapping. Liven up objects which are laying around the house – hat boxes, side tables, glass vases and metal containers are all suitable for decoration. In fact, découpage can be applied to any surface that will accept paper cut-outs and varnish.

Although the technique has been used in European folk art since the introduction of paper in the 12th century, découpage first became fashionable in Venice in the 17th century, when painted furniture was very much in vogue. Prints or original designs were mass-produced, then hand painted to be glued on to furniture and varnished so many times that the edges of the paper could not be felt. It was a cost-effective way of producing furniture which looked similar to the hand painted and highly lacquered original Japanese and Chinese pieces, which at the time were so prohibitively expensive to buy. This technique became known as arte povero or lacche povero which means 'poor man's lacquer'.

It next gained popularity with the ladies of the French court, who used special pasted prints of feathers, fans and fashion plates to decorate screens, boxes and furniture, finishing them off with as many as thirty coats of varnish. By the time Victoria was on the throne of England, découpage had become the hobby of ladies of leisure and gentlefolk throughout Europe. Kits were made available in ladies' magazines and special scrapbooks containing the motifs were very much in demand.

Today, découpage kits can be found in art shops, and if the traditional styles appeal to you, you will find them useful. However, equally effective material can be found in the printed material which surrounds us in every day life.

Materials & Equipment

OBJECTS TO WHICH DÉCOUPAGE CAN BE APPLIED

If you haven't tried this technique before, an inexpensive object with flat surfaces, such as a small cardboard box or a coaster is ideal. Once you have gained confidence, the world is your oyster.

Household items such as trays, bowls, boxes, pots and urns can be decorated; in fact, you will find many things to decorate already in your home without having to go out and buy them. As your skill increases you can progress to furniture; chairs, tables, chests, picture frames, doors, the list is endless. In fact, virtually anything with a smooth surface can be decorated with découpage.

PAPER TO USE FOR DÉCOUPAGE

Once you have found an object to decorate, the next step is to find suitable paper cut-outs. Remember, images that are in copyright cannot be used for découpage on objects produced for commercial purposes. However, the sources of material for découpage are vast and quite easily accessible – magazines, prints, greetings cards, gift wrapping, postcards, packaging, even music sheets and old maps.

Images that you wish to use, but which are in books too good to destroy, can be photocopied. Access to colour photocopiers is readily available in many high street shops and the quality of reproduction can be superb. If you use black and white photocopies, you can paint them or hand-tint them. This can be almost as effective (see Card Table).

A card or print that is too thick is best thinned before you attempt to stick it down. Wipe the back of it with a wet sponge and then carefully peel off the damp, back layer.

FIXATIVES

Depending on the quality of paper you are using, you may need to fix the image to protect it against bleeding and discolouration. Fixing the surface will turn a porous surface into a non-porous one. You will need a good spray fixative and you can choose between either a matt or gloss finish. It provides an acrylic-based coat which protects and minimizes the chances of the print turning yellow with age.

PAINTS

The object to which découpage is to be applied will dictate which type of paint to use as a base. Although oil-based paints give a more vibrant colour, water-based paints are actually easier to use.

Emulsion can be used on most surfaces and is water soluble. You will find that many of the pieces in this book are first painted with emulsion. Allow each coat to dry first before applying the next.

Acrylic paints are quick drying and are available in a huge range of colours. For detailed paint work, acrylics are ideal.

Gloss, enamel, ceramic and glass paints are designed for use on metal, glass and ceramic surfaces, as their names imply.

Spray paint is a simple way to apply colour, especially in tight corners or for unusual effects (see Cherub Magazine Rack).

ADHESIVES

Again, the object to which you are applying découpage will dictate which type of adhesive you use.

PVA, polyvinyl acetate woodworking glue, has been mostly used throughout the book. It is a multi-purpose glue and easy to use. Please note, that when it is first applied, it is a thick white paste, but it dries to

leave a clear, glossy finish. It can be diluted with water or used at full strength and can be used to seal wooden surfaces before glueing on the paper cut-outs.

Wallpaper paste is not as strong as PVA, but it is very pliable and can be used to stick and mould paper into and around awkward shapes. It enables the paper to be slightly stretched, but you need to be very careful when doing this to avoid tearing the paper.

Spray adhesive is clean and quick to use. It is ideal for repositioning and holding stencils in place. Direct it where needed and use in a well ventilated room.

Blu-Tack is a putty-like temporary adhesive which can be used to initially place and reposition your paper cut-outs enabling you to decide on a pleasing composition. The Blu-Tack can then be removed and replaced with a permanent adhesive.

Masking tape can be used to mask off sections when painting (see Airmail Drop-leaf Table). It is advisable to stick it onto a piece of fabric to remove most of the glue before it is used on a painted surface, otherwise it has a tendency to pull the paint off when you remove it .

VARNISHES

Varnishing is the final and most important aspect of découpage. It is used to protect the paper cut-out shapes, smooth the surface and give a lacquer-like finish.

Wood varnish, or clear polyurethane wood varnish, gives a good durable finish. It is available in matt, satin or gloss finishes, as well as in a variety of different tints.

Artist's acrylic varnish or picture varnish, although quite expensive, doesn't yellow with age.

PVA can be used to glue down the paper motifs. It can also be used to immediately coat the finished object, giving it a slightly shiny finish. When it is first applied it is white, but it dries to a transparent finish.

Découpage varnish is available in découpage kits and craft shops and is ideal for smaller objects, especially those painted with emulsion. It gives a shiny, luscious finish.

Crackle varnish is available together with crackle glaze to give a lacquered antique effect. It has been used for one project in this book (see Gardening Trunk).

For a background, if the effect to be achieved is of a colour showing through the cracks of another colour, two contrasting colours in emulsion are needed, as well as the crackle glaze and varnish.

Paint your object in one colour, and, when it is dry, paint over it with a thick layer of crackle glaze. Once that is dry, paint over it again with the second colour. Within seconds you will notice the paint cracking to reveal the first colour underneath. Glue on your chosen découpage motifs and apply a final coat of crackle glaze.

Wax can be used as a final touch after the varnishing has been completed. It should be applied when the varnish is completely dry to produce a lasting shine. Apply with a soft cloth in circular motions, leave to dry, then rub off. Repeat a couple of times until a satisfactory shine has developed.

USEFUL EQUIPMENT

Brushes You will need a selection of brushes: large or medium decorators' brushes to paint and varnish the larger surfaces, a child's craft brush to apply the glue to the pieces of découpage and fine artists' brushes for the detailed paint work.

Note: Clean brushes immediately after use and keep turpentine substitute/white spirit and water close at hand.

Scissors and craft knives It is a good idea to keep a pair of paper scissors, manicure scissors and a craft knife for cutting out. Keep them very sharp, otherwise the paper will tear. Use the scissors for the simple shapes and the manicure scissors and craft knife for the intricate details. If the paper is delicate fix it before you start to work on it.

Sandpaper may be needed to prepare surfaces before applying découpage and between layers of paint and varnish. When you sand surfaces in between layers of varnish, you will notice that they become white and grainy. Do not worry if this happens, this will disappear as the next coat is applied.

Rubber roller to use when glueing down paper. It is useful for pushing a glued print into position and ensuring that it lies flat without any air bubbles.

Access to a photocopier for use when the images you desire are in books that you do not wish to damage, and to reduce or enlarge them.

Basic Techniques

COMPOSITION

The art of découpage requires no drawing skills whatsoever, yet the finished result can be truly amazing.

Working out a composition involves placing cut-out shapes on your chosen object in a satisfying way. Using Blu-Tack, arrange the motifs until the desired effect is achieved, then remove the motifs one by one, replacing the Blu-Tack with permanent adhesive as you go along.

SEALING

Before anything is done to the chosen print, fix it with a spray fixative or diluted PVA . This will strengthen the paper, as well as protecting the image from bleeding, distorting and ageing.

PREPARING SURFACES

Should you wish to apply découpage to old items of wooden furniture with split wood or chipped paint, it may first be necessary to fill holes with wood filler before sanding and repainting it.

You may need to use wire wool to clean off any rust spots from old metal items. To clean metal, rinse off with one part vinegar to one part water.

Ceramics and glassware need little preparation apart from a wash in warm soapy water, to make sure that the surface is free of dust and grease.

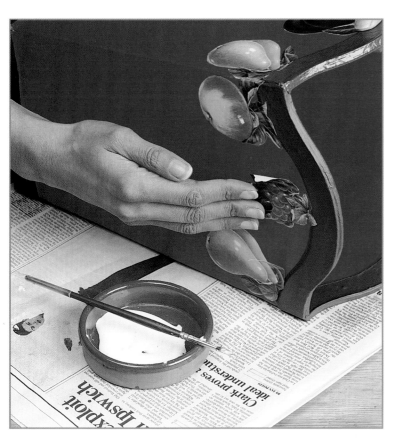

PRIMING

For most of the projects in this book the surfaces have first been cleaned and then painted. This makes the surfaces easier to work on and provides a simple unadorned view of the object prior to deciding how it should be decorated. Be sure to allow the first coat to dry before applying the next coat of paint.

CUTTING

Use a pair of paper scissors when you cut out the larger pieces and a pair of manicure scissors or a craft knife for the more intricate details. When using a craft knife, make sure that the blade is sharp, otherwise the paper will tear on the cutting board.

STICKING

When applying glue to the print, use a brush that is a suitable size for the paper – a fine brush for tiny cut-outs and a medium-sized decorator's brush for large ones. Once the paper is stuck onto the surface, cover it with a soft cloth and run a roller over it to release the air bubbles. If the roller does not seem to be making contact with the surface, rub over the cloth with your fingers.

VARNISHING

Varnish applied to découpage can range from three coats to thirty, depending on the effect that you wish to achieve. Ensure that the varnish is allowed to dry between coats in a dust-free environment.

To build up many coats, sand the surface after ten to twelve coats, clean with a damp cloth, then carry on varnishing. Do not sand the surface until you have at least ten coats of varnish. If the surface looks white and grainy when sanded, it will disappear with the next layer of varnish.

Sunflower Urn

This large black iron pot has been transformed from what once looked like a witch's cauldron to a bright and cheerful object. Although it cannot, in its new guise, be used as a cooking utensil, it now makes an ideal container for indoor plants.

YOU WILL NEED

Large iron pot
Black gloss and blue emulsion paints
Blu-Tack, PVA glue
Paintbrush, découpage varnish

1 Make sure that the pot is clean and dry before you paint it black.

2 Sponge the inside with blue paint.

3 Cut out sunflowers from gift wrap. Use Blu-tack to position them where you want them around the pot.

4 Glue the sunflowers onto the pot with PVA glue.

5 Finish the pot with découpage varnish.

15

Display Box

Show off your treasures or use as a tidy to store your make-up in this pretty box covered with tiny teapots, cups and saucers. Again, the motifs were found on gift wrapping paper, just one of the many different sources from which to obtain subjects for découpage.

YOU WILL NEED
Tray, pale blue emulsion paint, paintbrush
Scissors and/or craft knife, Blu-Tack, PVA glue
Découpage varnish

1 Paint the tray a colour to match the teapots, in this case a pale blue. Use two coats for a smooth finish.

2 Carefully cut out the motifs, using a craft knife to take out the insides of the cup and pot handles.

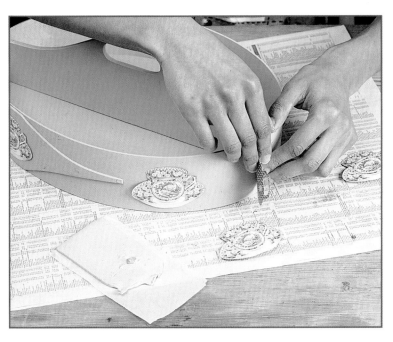

3 Glue down with PVA, pressing firmly and rubbing away any air bubbles as they occur.

4 Finish the box with découpage varnish.

Fruity Waste Paper Bin

The use of découpage can transform the most ordinary of household objects into something striking and original. This waste paper bin was originally a dull beige but is now as handsome as it is useful.

YOU WILL NEED
Waste paper bin, fruit motifs
2 x paintbrushes, one very fine
Dark green and red emulsion paint
PVA glue, découpage varnish

1 Using dark green emulsion, paint the upper and lower rims of the waste paper bin with a fine brush.

2 With the red emulsion, paint the rest of the bin inside and out, avoiding the green edging.

3 Cut out the fruit motifs, these were taken from a découpage kit.

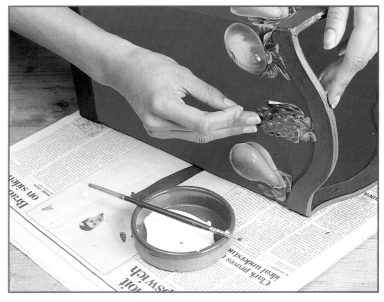

4 Arrange the fruits around the top of the bin making sure that the leaves blend into the green paint. Glue down with PVA and finish off with découpage varnish.

Gardening Tools Trunk

This old tin trunk is just the right size to hold gardening bits and pieces, so it would be a nice idea to extend the gardening theme to the exterior. We have decorated it with a green crackle effect and découpage in the form of seed packets and gardening labels.

YOU WILL NEED
Dark and light green emulsion paints
Acrylic crackle varnish
Acrylic crackle glaze
Medium-sized paintbrushes
Seed packets and labels, old trunk

1 Paint the trunk dark green, leave to dry and then paint with a thick layer of crackle glaze.

2 Once the crackle glaze is dry, paint over it with a layer of light green. Within minutes, the paint will crackle to reveal the dark green underneath. Allow to dry.

3 Select your seed packets and gardening labels and glue them at random onto the trunk using PVA glue.

4 Once this is dry, apply a final coat of crackle varnish.

Leaf Lampshade

Books of old botanical prints are a good source of subjects for découpage. In this case, we have chosen acanthus leaves, often incorporated into architectural forms, to decorate this rather ordinary plastic lampshade. A black-and-white photocopier was used to capture the images which were then coloured in.

YOU WILL NEED
Lampshade, PVA glue, green paint, paintbrush
Shiny polyurethane varnish
Watercolour paint in lime green

1 Photocopy the leaves, adjusting the sizes to fit the lampshade.

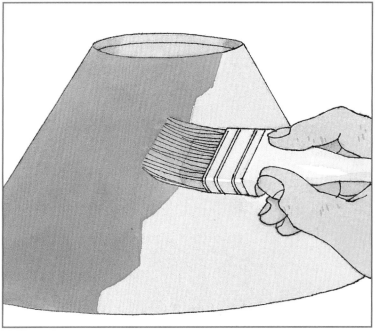

2 Paint the lampshade with dark green emulsion paint and leave to dry.

3 Paint the photocopied leaves with a lime green wash. Arrange the leaves round the lampshade using Blu-Tack.

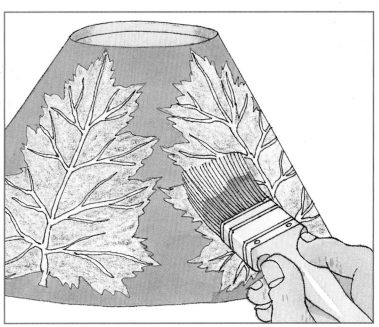

4 With PVA glue, stick the leaves in position, leaving to dry. Coat the whole outer shade with the varnish.

Seashell Mirror and Bath Brush Set

The natural wood finish of the mirror and bath brush offset the beautiful colours of the shell print that was found in a magazine. Arrange these bathroom accessories among your own shell collection, and create a seaside haven in the corner of your bathroom.

YOU WILL NEED
Wooden bath brush and hand mirror
Scissors, Blu-Tack, PVA glue
Wood varnish and print fixative

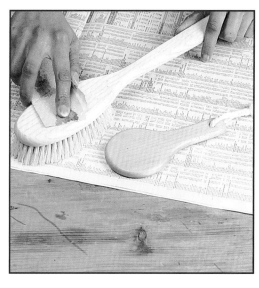

1 Using a colour photocopier, reduce your chosen pictures to fit the backs of the mirror and brush. Cut out.

2 Spray with fixative to ensure that the print will not distort when dampened with glue.

3 Sand the wooden surfaces, so that the wood will accept the glue and varnish.

4 Arrange the shell motifs around the brush and mirror, using Blu-Tack for easy positioning. Then glue into place with PVA glue.

5 Give each piece three coats of wood varnish, leaving to dry thoroughly between coats.

Heavenly Magazine Rack

Little cherubs stand guard over your newspapers and journals as well as keeping them tidy in this heavenly magazine rack. Cherubs and putti have always been a popular theme, especially in fine art and traditional découpage.

YOU WILL NEED
Plain wooden magazine rack
Sky blue emulsion paint, paintbrush
White spray paint, scissors, PVA glue
Wood varnish

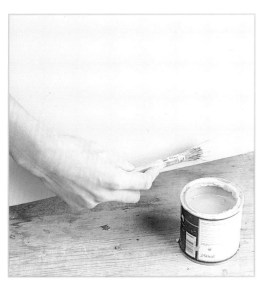

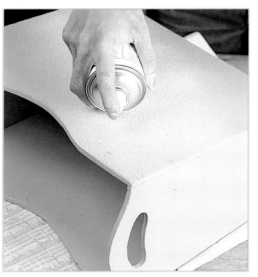

1 Paint the magazine rack with sky blue emulsion, ideally using two coats for a smooth finish.

2 With white spray paint, spray in a group of fluffy clouds onto one side of the rack.

3 On a colour photocopier, enlarge the cherubs (taken from an illustration) to the right size and cut them out.

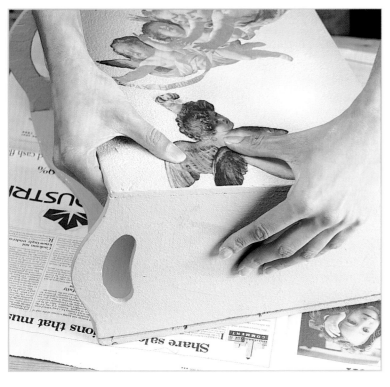

4 Arrange the cherubs on the magazine rack and glue in place with PVA glue.

5 Give each piece three coats of wood varnish, leaving to dry thoroughly between coats.

Angel Boxes

Angels are another popular theme with enthusiasts of découpage. The angels used on these trinket boxes came from a widely-available découpage kit. Paint the boxes and if, like these, they fit into one another, paint them in alternate celestial colours.

YOU WILL NEED
A selection of trinket boxes
Emulsion paint in turquoise, pink and lilac
PVA glue, paintbrush, scissors
Découpage varnish

1 Cut out small and large angel faces acquired from a bought kit or other source.

2 Paint the boxes and the lids with two coats of emulsion in turquoise, pink and lilac. Leave to dry.

3 Using Blu-Tack, arrange the angels on the boxes according to colour, putting the large angels on the lids.

4 Stick the angels in place using PVA glue.

5 Coat the boxes with découpage varnish.

To make papier mâché

Roughly tear up pieces of
newspaper about 1 inch square.
Prepare some wallpaper paste
according to the manufacturer's
instructions. Dip the paper into
the paste and stick onto the letter
rack, graduallybuilding it up
as you go along. Leave to dry
thoroughly.

Celestial Desk Set

This attractive desk set consisting of pencil pot, mock book box and home-made papier mâché letter rack have been painted and covered with colour photocopies of beautiful antique maps of the heavens. The pot was bought, though half a squeezy bottle will work just as well. The book box is available from most craft or hobby shops.

YOU WILL NEED
Pencil pot, or half a plastic bottle
Book box, heavy card for the letter rack
(a rectangular shape for the base, and three semi-circles each smaller than the next)
Strips of newspaper and wallpaper paste (for the papier mâché)
Paints in red, blue and green, paintbrushes
PVA glue, scissors, découpage varnish

2 Paint the pencil pot red and the book box blue. Give two coats to each and allow to dry thoroughly.

3 Colour-photocopy the celestial images out of a book, reduce to the correct size. Cut out carefully

1 To make the letter rack, tape the semi-circles to the rectangular shaped base, the largest at the back, then the middle-sized, then the small. Then cover it in papier mâché, at least four of five coats, to make it sturdy and straight. Leave to dry and paint it green.

4 Glue the pieces into position using PVA, when coat with découpage varnish to give a lacquered finish.

Mosaic Vase

An ingenious way to transform an old vase is to cover it in a paper mosaic. The vase can be any shape or size; the paper you choose could be subtle and elegant or bold and dramatic. We have used a sedate floral gift wrap, but suitable images can be taken from other sources.

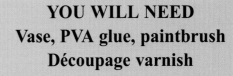

YOU WILL NEED
Vase, PVA glue, paintbrush
Découpage varnish

1 Choose a paper which is large enough to cover the surface of the vase. Check first by wrapping it loosely around.

2 Tear the paper into irregular pieces, keeping them in order to make it easy to piece the mosaic together.

3 Assemble the torn pieces onto the vase, glueing them on as you go along with PVA glue.

4 When the vase is entirely covered with the paper, leave to dry and then cover the vase with a coat of découpage varnish.

Ski Resort Coasters

These coasters are reminiscent of souvenirs available in tourist shops the world over. Use your old skiing maps to recreate these pleasantly kitsch versions. Pages from local street maps would be just as effective if you overlay them with pictures of places of local interest.

1 Select the area you wish to use on the map, place coaster over the top and draw around it.

2 Carefully cut around the circle using a sharp pair of scissors.

3 Glue map down onto the coaster and trim off excess, if necessary, with a craft knife,

4 Cut out figures or sections of locations you wish to superimpose and glue onto the coaster.

5 Paint the edge of the coaster with white paint. Leave to dry and coat the whole with découpage varnish.

Victorian Photograph Album

The sources of some of the most popular images in découpage are borrowed from Victoriana. Pictures of wasp-waisted ladies with parasols, fans, flowers and feathers are the most commonly seen and often included in découpage sets. This would be a good first project for people new to the technique.

YOU WILL NEED
Dark, antique-looking photo album
Victorian découpage kit (feathers and flowers)
Scissors, PVA glue

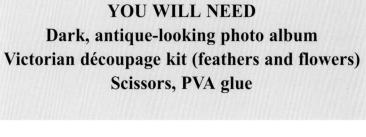

1 Select a number of fans, feathers and flowers from a Victorian-style découpage kit. Alternatively, you could cut out images from gift wrap.

2 Arrange cut-outs on the front cover of the photograph album.

3 Stick down with PVA glue, wiping over it with a soft cloth to remove any air bubbles.

4 If the cover of the photo album is vinyl, don't varnish. A fabric cover will, however, accept découpage varnish.

Cup Cake Flower Pots

Terra-cotta flower pots have great potential for decoration. They come in good strong shapes and have a surface which will accept paint well. When covered with découpage and varnished they are totally transformed from their original form.

YOU WILL NEED
Lilac and green emulsion paint
Paintbrush, PVA glue, Blu-Tack
Scissors, découpage varnish

1 Wash and dry the flower pot, then give it a couple of coats of emulsion, leaving the first coat to dry before starting the next.

2 From gift wrap paper, cut out the pictures (in this case, cup cakes) carefully.

3 Using Blu-Tack, evenly position the images along the bottom edge of the flower pot.

4 Stick down, using PVA glue. Then coat with découpage varnish, to give the pot an attractive smooth sheen and protect the pictures.

Starry Glass Bottles

A simple way to create elegant bottles from any old ones you may have lying around at home. The ones used here are aromatherapy oil bottles made out of blue glass.

YOU WILL NEED
Blue bottles, gold wax gilt, soft cloth
Gummed gold stars (available from stationers)

1 Make sure that the bottles are clean – wash and dry thoroughly.

2 Remove the stars from their backing paper and arrange on the bottles.

3 Rub a tiny amount of gold wax gilt into the tops of the cork stoppers using a soft cloth. Seal with PVA glue.

Canny Containers

These tin cans once held beans and tomatoes, but can be given a new purpose in life once the labels have been removed, the cans painted, and a motif added. They are ideal for storing pens and pencils, or can be used as cache-pots.

YOU WILL NEED
Tin cans, masking tape
Emulsion paint (pink, turquoise, orange)
Paintbrush, craft knife, scissors
PVA glue, découpage varnish

1 Peel labels off cans, and making sure that they are clean, mask off area large enough to fit the motif.

2 Paint cans using emulsion paint. Use 2-3 coats, waiting for each coat to dry before applying the next.

3 Remove the masking tape carefully and scrape off any excess paint from the edges with your craft knife.

4 Cut out your motifs (we used Indian postcards) and glue into position with PVA glue.

5 Coat the entire surface of each can with découpage varnish.

Smart Shoe Box

Shoe boxes are wonderful space savers enabling you to tidy up your letters, cassettes, pencils – even your shoes. We have entirely covered one in wrapping paper bearing a most appropriate design: the other has been covered with scraps of tissue and sugar paper.

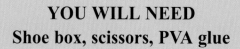
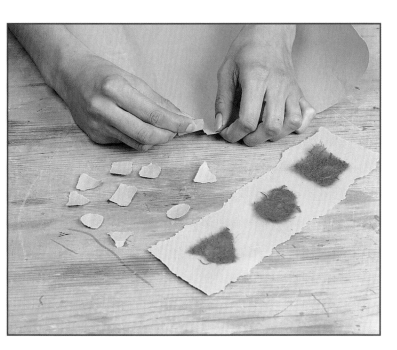

1 For the tissue-covered version, place the lid of the box onto the piece of tissue paper, right side down, and cut the paper as shown in the picture.

2 Glue down the inside edges with PVA glue.

3 Using sugar paper in a contrasting colour, tear out large rectangle and small geometric shapes for the lid and edges.

4 Tear larger geometric shapes out of tissue paper and stick in the centre of the sugar paper rectangle. Then with PVA glue, stick the whole thing on to the lid. Stick the smaller shapes around the edges.

Madonna and Child Mirror

This mirror was originally an old wooden frame which has been painted and decorated with religious images taken from Christmas cards. The frame looks rich and sumptuous and would look perfect in a hallway.

YOU WILL NEED
Old wooden picture frame
Scissors/craft knife, PVA glue
Découpage varnish, small paintbrush
Gold powder, Blu-Tack, wire wool

1 From a selection of old Christmas cards, select the images you require and cut them out carefully.

2 Rub the inner frame with wire wool and then apply a tiny amount of gold powder with a soft cloth, working it into the wood grain.

3 Using Blu-Tack, position your images into the corners of the frame, trimming to fit. Stick into position with PVA glue.

4 Position the smaller images around the frame and glue down firmly.

5 Coat the whole frame with découpage varnish. This will protect the images and the gold powder finish.

Gold-Leaf and Sweet Wrapper Lampshade

A cream fabric lampshade is given the rags-to-riches treatment with the simple application of gold-leaf, wrappers from your favourite sweets and a tea-bag. From humble beginnings, it is transformed into a luxurious gilded table lamp.

YOU WILL NEED
Cream or white fabric lampshade, gold-leaf
PVA glue, paintbrush, gold wax gilt, soft cloth
Damp tea-bag

1 Cut the gold-leaf roughly into quarters. Paint diluted PVA (1 part water, 1 part PVA) on the the areas of the shade where you wish to lay the gold-leaf.

2 Carefully remove the gold-leaf backing and place on to the shade. Allow to dry.

3 Rub over gently with a fingernail to distress.

4 Tear foil sweet wrappers into small triangles and glue them down between the gold-leaf. Rub over the whole shade with a damp tea-bag to give a sepia tinge to the shade.

5 Apply gold wax gilt to the upper and lower shade edges, using a soft cloth.

Leaf Cassette Cabinet

This cardboard cassette box, though originally quite plain, has been turned into a repository for a variety of natural dried leaves. It has been interspersed with aluminium leaves and silver-leaf to create an autumnal space saver.

YOU WILL NEED
Cassette box, silver-leaf, pressed leaves
Leaves cut from a tomato purée tube
PVA glue, paintbrush, découpage varnish

1 Paint the fronts of the drawers with diluted PVA. Carefully remove the silver-leaf backing and cover the fronts of the drawers with it.

2 Once dry, distress by rubbing the surfaces with a fingernail. Repeat on all the drawers.

3 Cut out some leaf shapes from the tomato purée tube and arrange, together with the genuine pressed leaves, on the cabinet surround.

4 Stick the leaves into position with PVA glue.

5 Once the leaves are dry, coat the entire cabinet with découpage varnish.

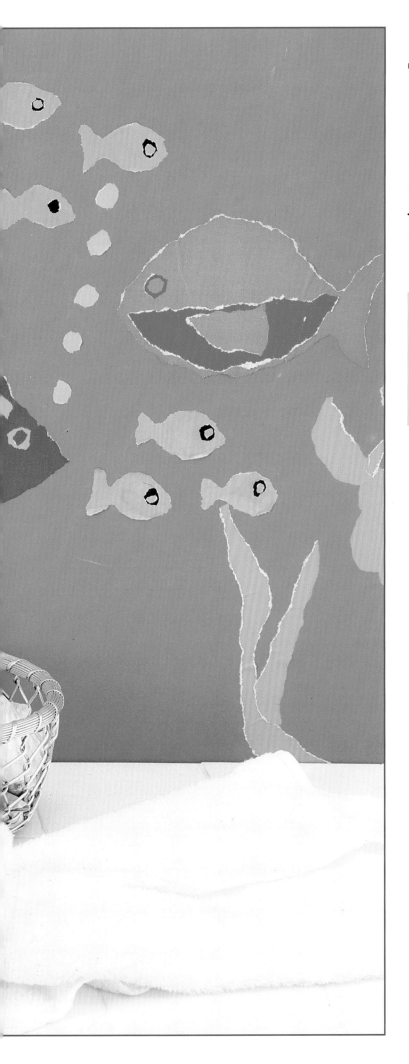

Aquarium Wall

This is a good way of livening up your bathroom wall or, in fact, any wall in your home. Torn paper can be most effective if the shapes you choose are simple and the colours bright. Fish are just the kind of simple shapes you need and look effective in large groups surrounded by marine vegetation and other denizens of the deep.

YOU WILL NEED
Glossy paper in bright colours, bright blue paint for the wall (emulsion or vinyl)
PVA glue, découpage varnish

1 Paint the wall bright blue with two coats of paint, or as many as needed to produce a smooth finish and good depth of colour.

2 Choose some brightly coloured glossy paper and on the reverse side draw out some simple fish shapes.

5 With Blu-Tack, position your fish over the wall, along with the air bubbles and weed.

3 Now tear out the fish shapes and the details in contrasting colours. Don't be too cautious when you are doing this for sometimes mistakes work out well – once you have tried it you will realize how easy it is.

4 Also tear out strips for vegetation and small circles for air bubbles. With PVA glue, stick the contrasting detail on to the fish shapes.

6 Once you have positioned the fish to your liking, glue them down with PVA. Once this is done, varnish the entire wall with découpage varnish.

Card Table

A glass-topped table already has a built-in advantage where découpage is concerned. Remove the top and the range of objects that can be laid underneath is vast – stamps, foreign bank notes, postcards and photographs. We have created a games table by using playing cards.

YOU WILL NEED
Round glass-topped table, black emulsion
Large decorator's brush, fine brush
Playing cards, acrylic paints, scissors

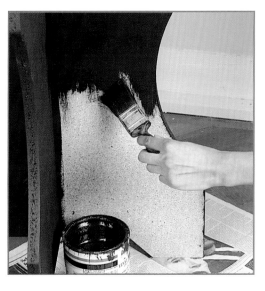

1 Remove the glass top and paint the table black.

2 Photocopy 12 picture cards from a pack, or use some antique examples – we found these in a book.

3 If you are using black and white photocopies, paint in the colours using the acrylic paints.

4 Once the paint on the cards is dry, arrange them on the table top.

5 When the desired effect is achieved, replace the glass.

Floral Ottoman

This linen chest was made from a do-it-yourself kit and to avoid the mass-produced look has been given some individuality of its own with a floral découpage design. The flowers were taken from gift wrap.

YOU WILL NEED
Do-it-yourself ottoman kit
Scissors and craft knife, PVA glue, Blu-Tack
Paintbrush, wood varnish

1 From your chosen wrapping paper, cut out as many individual flowers as possible, neatening with a craft knife.

2 Using Blu-Tack, arrange the flowers on the front panel of the ottoman.

3 Using PVA glue, stick the flowers in position. By layering them, a 3-D effect can be achieved. Leave to dry.

4 To match the glossy finish of the rest of the chest, and for protection, coat the panel with découpage varnish.

Drop-Leaf Airmail Table

This larger than life drop-leaf table, decorated to resemble an airmail letter, is a quirky, amusing way to rejuvenate a shabby old table into an interesting piece of furniture ideal for a child or teenager's room.

YOU WILL NEED
Table, masking tape, paintbrushes
PVA glue, wood varnish
Emulsion paint (sky blue, navy blue, red

1 Paint the table with the sky blue emulsion, using 2-3 coats.

2 Mask off the edges of the table in short, diagonal stripes, similar to the edges of an airmail envelope.

3 Paint each masked section, red and navy blue alternately. Allow to dry and remove the tape very carefully.

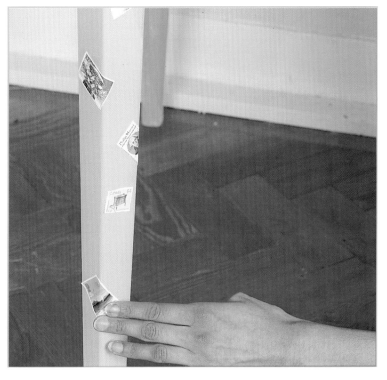

4 Taking the words *Par avion* from an airmail envelope and a stamp, enlarge up on a colour photocopier. Cut out and glue onto the table.

5 Glue old stamps onto the legs of the table and coat the entire thing with varnish.

Musical Hat Box

Hat boxes are such lovely shapes and just cry out to be decorated in beautiful and interesting ways. Here, we have photocopied sheet music superimposed with pictures of cherubs from out of a book and stained it with tea to produce an antique effect.

YOU WILL NEED
Tea-bag, PVA glue, scissors
Découpage varnish

1 Take the images of your choice and photocopy them. Soak one tea-bag in warm water. Wring it out slightly and drag it over the photocopy until covered. Leave to dry.

2 Join enough pieces of music together to cover the hat box and lid. Fold in half an inch along the bottom and snip at intervals to make turning under easier. For the lid, cut a circle with ½ inch extra all round, snip to turn. Cut a strip for the rim.

3 Using PVA glue, cover the bottom and lid. Finish off the lid by adding the strip around the rim.

4 Coat the entire outside of the box and lid with découpage varnish.

Gingham Daisy Cabinet

Liven up your bedroom with this bedside cabinet – we have chosen sunny yellow paint and gingham daisies to wake you up with a smile. However, this design can be varied. You could, perhaps, copy part of your wallpaper design or vary the colour according to your bedroom colour scheme.

YOU WILL NEED
Old bedside cabinet, yellow emulsion paint
Paintbrush, yellow gingham, calico
Orange Dylon pen, PVA glue, scissors, paper

1 Paint the cabinet with two coats of bright yellow emulsion paint and leave to dry.

2 Draw out paper templates for two different-sized flowers (the smaller for the drawer and door, the larger for the cabinet surrounds). Cut them out, place on fabric and draw around them. Also draw some flower centres.

3 Cut out the flowers, glueing the centres onto the petals with PVA glue. Draw around the edge of the flower with a Dylon pen, to give the flowers a sharp outline.

4 Glue the flowers onto the cabinet with PVA, placing the smaller ones on the drawer and the door and the larger on the cabinet surrounds. Finally glue daisy onto handle.

Glass Rose Bowl

This flowery bowl is inspired by the decorated glassware of the 1950s and began life as an ordinary, unembellished mixing bowl. It has been transformed with a découpage kit and gloss paint.

YOU WILL NEED
Glass mixing bowl, white and green gloss paints
Sponge, paintbrushes, roses découpage kit
Scissors, masking tape, PVA glue, print fixative

1 Cut out your chosen motifs and spray them with print fixative.

2 Brush PVA glue onto the front of the image and firmly stick onto the outside of the bowl with the picture facing in.

3 Once the glue is dry, mask off the top edge of the bowl and then paint the outside of the bowl with white gloss paint. Do the first coat with a sponge so that the paint stays put. When the first coat is dry, paint the second coat on with a brush.

4 When the white paint is completely dry, paint over it with green paint. Do several coats, leaving each coat to dry before starting the next. Remove the masking tape.

Love Hearts Box

There are so many beautiful gift wrap papers available that it is a crime to use them only for wrapping presents. When you come across a paper that you particularly like, such as this one with heart motifs, keep it to use for découpage.

1 Mask off the edge of the lid, and using gold paint, spray the lid so that the centre is denser that the edges. Remove the masking tape.

2 Cut out the hearts from the gift wrap, smaller ones for the edge of the lid and larger ones for the lid and the base.

3 Position the small hearts around the rim of the lid and one large heart on the top. Stick with PVA glue.

4 Position the rest of the hearts around the base, joining them together so that none of the original box shows. Glue down, wiping with a soft cloth to remove air bubbles.

5 When dry, coat the entire box with découpage varnish.

Fruity Chest of Drawers

This chest of drawers started life as a do-it-yourself kit from a large furniture store. With the help of some large colour photocopies taken from a book of Victorian botanical prints, the drawers have been transformed into something special.

YOU WILL NEED
Chest of drawers, scissors, PVA glue
Blu-Tack, paintbrush, wood varnish

1 Select your pictures from a book or magazine – botanical prints are a good source of material. Colour photocopy to the required size.

2 With a pair of scissors or a craft knife, carefully cut out the images.

3 Using Blu-Tack, arrange the fruit on the front of the drawers.

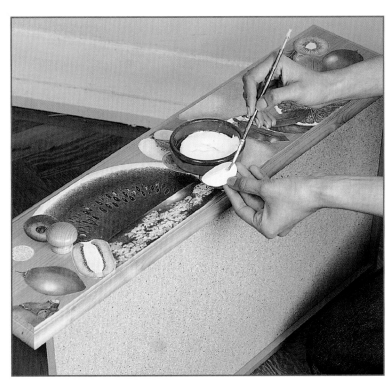

4 Using PVA glue, stick down your arrangement and leave to dry.

5 Coat the front of the drawers with wood varnish.

Flower Candles

The concept behind these decorated candles is not, strictly speaking, découpage, but the method of application is. If you prefer to use pictures instead of pressed flowers, the method is exactly the same.

YOU WILL NEED
Large wax candles, pressed flowers, PVA glue
Saucepan, paintbrush, wax

1 Choose a selection of flowers and press for a few days until they are thoroughly dry.

2 Position each flower onto the candle using PVA glue. Take care not to use too much.

3 Melt some wax in a saucepan. Spoon the hot wax over the flowers to seal them into position. Leave in a dry place for a few days to harden.

Window Box

Découpage can be applied to a plastic window box, and can safely be used outside, as long as you put layers of varnish on it to protect it against inclement weather.

YOU WILL NEED
Green plastic window box
PVA glue, scissors, clear acrylic varnish
Glue brush, coloured paper squares

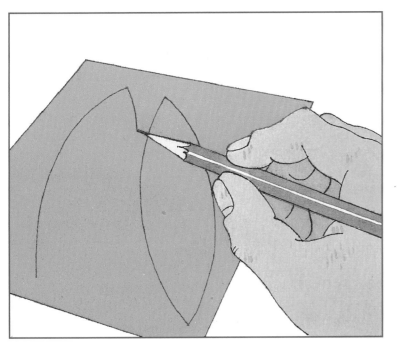

1 On the back of green paper squares draw simple leaf shapes. Carefully rip along the lines you have just drawn and don't worry about unevenness – it adds to the design.

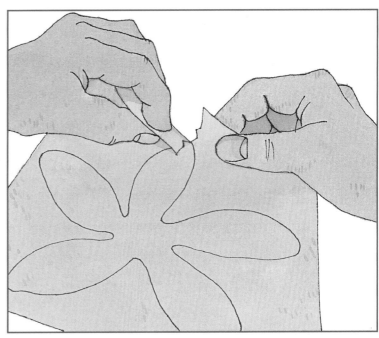

2 Repeat the process for the flowers, and tear out some circles in contrasting colours for the flower centres.

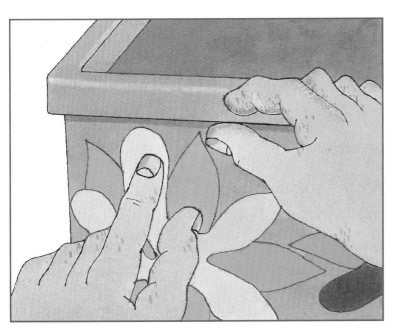

3 With the PVA glue, stick the leaves onto the window box, followed by the flowers and then their centres.

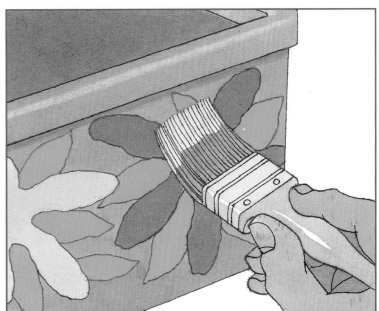

4 When completely dry, paint on clear acrylic varnish and leave to dry between coats. Use at least 5 coats of varnish.

Jungle Animals Lampshade

A plain wicker lampshade has been given the exotic treatment with jungle animals sauntering around it. Again, these images were found on wrapping paper and carefully cut out. If you don't use up all the animals on the shade, decorate the base as well.

YOU WILL NEED
Plain wicker lampshade, scissors
Craft knife, PVA glue
Blu-Tack, découpage varnish

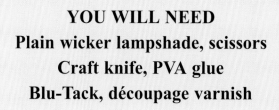

1 Carefully cut out the individual animals from the paper. Use a craft knife where the outline is intricate.

2 Using Blu-Tack, position the animals along both edges of the shade, as if they are walking around them.

3 When you are happy with the positioning, glue down with PVA.

4 Paint the shade with découpage varnish.

Farmyard Plate

This decorative object was once an ordinary enamel camping plate. Découpage has been applied to it in the form of farmyard animals and the grass has been painted in. Please note that this is now strictly for decoration. Do not eat from it.

YOU WILL NEED
Enamel plate, scissors, Blu-Tack, PVA glue
Fine paintbrush, dark green acrylic paint
Découpage varnish

1 Make sure that the plate is clean – wash in warm soapy water and dry thoroughly. Choose your animals and position them around the edge of the plate using Blu-Tack. Re-position until they are evenly placed. Using PVA glue, stick the animals onto the plate.

2 Using dark green acrylic paint, paint the edges to resemble grass.

3 Cover the plate with découpage varnish.

Farmyard Coat Peg

This coat peg uses the same farmyard animals as for the enamel plate on the previous page.
It is not only functional, but a decorative addition to a child's bedroom.